No Boys Allowed

No Boys Allowed

Poems About Brothers and Sisters

Compiled by John Micklos, Jr.

Illustrations by Kathleen O'Malley

Boyds Mills Press

To siblings everywhere, who laugh together, share dreams together, and create memories together

J. M., Jr.

Collection copyright © 2006 by John Micklos, Jr.
Illustrations copyright © 2006 by Kathleen O'Malley
All rights reserved

Published by Wordsong
Boyds Mills Press, Inc.
A Highlights Company
815 Church Street
Honesdale, Pennsylvania 18431
Printed in China

Publisher Cataloging-in-Publication Data (U.S.)

Micklos, John, Jr.
No boys allowed : poems about brothers and sisters / by John Micklos, Jr. ;
illustrated by Kathleen O'Malley. —1st ed.
[32]p. : col. ill. ; cm.
Summary: Poems in celebration of siblings.
ISBN 1-59078-051-5
1. Siblings—poetry. 2. Brothers and sisters—Poetry. 3. American poetry—Collections.
I. O'Malley, Kathleen, ill. II. Title.

First edition, 2006
The text of this book is set in 15-point Berkeley.
The illustrations are done in watercolor.

Visit our Web site at www.boydsmillspress.com

10 9 8 7 6 5 4 3 2 1

Table of Contents

New Baby Sister

Tiny fingers,
Tiny toes,
Tiny little button nose—
That's my baby sister.

Tiny gurgles,
Tiny sighs,
Tiny little hungry cries—
That's my baby sister.

Too small to smile,
Too small to play,
Up all night, asleep all day—
That's my baby sister.

Sometimes she's a bother.
But I guess that's allowed,
'Cause she's still awfully cute,
And I'm still awfully proud.

John Micklos, Jr.

Little

I am the sister of him
And he is my brother.
He is too little for us
To talk to each other.

So every morning I show him
My doll and my book;
But every morning he still is
Too little to look.

Dorothy Aldis

I'm Still Getting Used to My Little Brother

Do I have to have a little brother?
That's all I want to know,
'cause to tell you the truth
he won't be much fun
until he starts to grow.
But by that time, I'll be bigger, too,
and I won't want him following me.
Yet I can see it already—
the way that he smiles—
just how my life will be.
He points and laughs and gets excited
whenever I just walk by.
He throws me his ball, *his toys, his food,*
and tries to get me to play.
The thing of it is,
he's kind of cute
in that baby sort of way.
I guess he's OK—after all,
it's clear that he adores me.
And I'd rather have him
than some other kid brother
who only just ignores me.

Allan A. De Fina

8

You and Me

Listen to the baby laugh!
When I was a baby, I did that.
His skin's so soft. His hair's so fine.
I know my numbers up to nine.
See how high he kicks his feet?
Yesterday I lost two teeth.

Grandma says he's sweet as jam.
Look and see how tall I am.
He looks just like a little elf.
I can tie all by myself.
Shhh . . . he's finally sleeping, see?
Hurray! It's time for you and me!

Rebecca Kai Dotlich

My Little Sister

My little sister
Likes to eat.
But when she does
She's not too neat.
The trouble is
She doesn't know
Exactly where
The food should go!

William Wise

Song of Frustration

I have a sister who writes on walls
And rides her tricycle through the halls
And drowns her dolls in the bathroom sink
And takes the last of the orange drink
And sucks her thumb and screams at bugs
And hides her sandwiches under the rugs
And rips my books and won't take naps
And always sits on the company's laps.

I have a sister who's almost four.
Sometimes I wish that she lived next door.

Lois Duncan

My Brother

My brother is
　　a redwood,
wedged between my toes.

My brother is
　　a basketball,
jammed up in my nose.

My brother is
　　a scratchy coat,
cut too small to fit.

My brother's
　　a mosquito,
just begging to get hit.

My brother is
　　a chain saw,
that once started whines and roars.

My brother is
　　the chicken pox.
He cannot be ignored.

Sara Holbrook

No Boys Allowed

There are absolutely,
Positively,
Without a doubt,
No boys allowed in my room.

No boys from school,
Or boys from church,
Or boys from the neighborhood,
Or even famous boys from
television shows.

No policemen,
Or firemen,
Or even my dad,
Or even the President.

And *especially*
No little brothers
Are ever, Ever, EVER
Allowed in my room,
No matter how hard you beg,
No matter how hard you plead,
No matter what you say.

Hey, I'm a little lonely now.
Want to come in and play?

John Micklos, Jr.

little sister
holds on tight.
My hands hurt
from all that squeezing,
but I don't mind.
She thinks no one will bother her
when I'm around,
and they won't
if I can help it.
And even when I can't,
I try
'cause she believes in me.

Nikki Grimes

Don't You Tease My Sister

Don't you tease my sister.
Don't call her silly names.
Don't push or punch or make her cry.
Don't leave her out of games.

Don't you tease my sister.
Don't try to make her sad.
'Cause when I see that she's upset
It really makes me mad!

I know *I* tease my sister.
That's normal as can be.
But if *you* tease my sister,
You'll have to deal with *me*.

John Micklos, Jr.

15

My Brother Loves Small Animals

My brother loves small animals,
especially birds.
Three times he brought home
baby swallows and nursed them.
He placed them in a shoebox
half-filled with cotton
and fed them milk with a water dropper.
He would gently move the wings
(to keep the muscles lively).
A few times I would help,
but it was hard
because I had to be
so careful with the
baby birds—and I
am so small myself.

Emanuel di Pasquale

The Two of Us

Dragging blankets,
rugs, and chairs,
we build a fort
beneath the stairs.
Then from the hall
our small platoon
stomps through each
and every room.
I stand guard,
he leads the way
in search of secret
passageways,
exploring new
and dangerous ground.
("Shhhhh!" he says. "Don't make a sound!")
From foreign shores
to castle towers;
so it goes in winter hours.

Rebecca Kai Dotlich

Hide and Go Seek

Little sister
thinks that
tree will
hide her.
It is slender;
she is wider.
I pretend
not to see
a very
odd tree
with an

    e
   l
bow

and a
    k
       n
      e e

Kristine O'Connell George

18

Sister and Bro

Emma and Teddy
Were sister and bro.
Everywhere Emma went,
Teddy would go.
Everywhere Teddy went,
Emma would not.
"Teddy," said Emma,
"I must have forgot."

Teddy and Emma
Were brother and sis.
Everything Emma did,
Teddy would miss.
Everything Emma did,
Teddy would say,
"Emma forgot me
Again today."

J. Patrick Lewis

Half-Whole-Step

I *have* a half-sister
I *have* a whole-sister
I *have* a step-sister
That adds up to three.

I *am* a half-brother
I *am* a whole-brother
I *am* a step-brother
There's just one of me!

Mary Ann Hoberman

Big Sister, Good-bye

My sister's leaving home today
to go to college far away.
She says she'll call.
She says she'll write.
She says she'll think of me each night.
But, oh, the world seems gloomy, gray.
My sister's leaving home today.

Eileen Spinelli

21

Who Ate the Last Five Cookies?

My sister said, "I couldn't!"
So I said, "I'm sure you could."

She said, "I really shouldn't!"
And I said, "I think you should."

She said, "You know I wouldn't!"
But I said, "I bet you would."

So when she said, "I didn't!"
I said, "Mama, yes she did!"

I was bad and I admit it.
(Just don't tell her where I've hid.)

David L. Harrison

I'm Telling

You looked at me!
You looked at me!
Don't say that it's not true!
It hurt so bad
     when you looked at me,
I think I'll tell on you!

Jane Medina

My Older Sister's in the Bathroom

How long do I
have to wait
my turn
outside this door?
If you don't
hurry *up* and *out*,
there'll be a puddle
on the floor!

Allan A. De Fina

The Quarrel

I quarreled with my brother
I don't know what about,
One thing led to another
And somehow we fell out.
The start of it was slight,
The end of it was strong,
He said he was right,
I knew he was wrong!

We hated one another.
The afternoon turned black.
Then suddenly my brother
Thumped me on the back,
And said, "Oh, *come* along!
We can't go on all night—
I was in the wrong."
So he was in the right.

Eleanor Farjeon

Birthday

Today I'm a year older
and he isn't.
I'm getting closer all the time.
If he skipped just two birthdays
while I was catching up,
we'd be even.
It wouldn't be so tough on him.
I'd give him presents anyway.

Richard J. Margolis

Lil' Bro'

I have to take my little brother
everywhere I go
'cause I'm his big sister
and Mama told me to.

His nose is always snotty
and his shoes come all untied,
his diapers get wet and dirty,
and he sure does like to cry.

He gets in the dirt
and runs in the street
and he doesn't like to mind—
but he's my little brother
and I keep him all the time.

Karama Fufuka

Sweet Dreams

It's always been a wish of mine
(Or should I say a dream)
To scare my sister half to death
And hear her piercing scream.

That's why I squished four bugs until
They all were very dead,
Then took them to my sister's room
And put them in her bed.

After we had said goodnight,
My heart began to pound.
I waited and I waited, but
She never made a sound.

And then I got so doggone tired
I couldn't stay awake.
I climbed into my own warm bed
And shrieked—there was a snake!

It wiggled, and I leaped and fell
And bruised my bottom half;
Then I heard an awful sound—
It was my sister's laugh.

Joyce Armor

Bunk Bed Dreams

When the hour is late
And the dark grows deep,
And even our parents
Are fast asleep,
We share our bunk bed dreams.

We whisper of things
That we plan to do.
You tell me your hopes;
I tell mine to you—
Sharing our bunk bed dreams.

We talk of the future,
Of riches and fame,
Of starring in movies
Or World Series games—
Sharing our bunk bed dreams.

For now they are secret,
Between me and you.
We whisper and wonder
If they will come true.
Sharing our bunk bed dreams.

John Micklos, Jr.

About the Poets

Dorothy Aldis was a noted children's writer whose books ranged from poetry to biography. "Little," her poem in this book, comes from her own book of poems *Everything and Anything.*

Joyce Armor is the author of many poems for children. "Sweet Dreams" first appeared in the book *Kids Pick the Funniest Poems: Poems That Make Kids Laugh,* selected by Bruce Lansky.

Allan A. De Fina is a professor of education at New Jersey City University, Jersey City, New Jersey. He is also a widely published poet whose books include *When a City Leans Against the Sky.* "I'm Still Getting Used to My Little Brother" and "My Older Sister's in the Bathroom" are original poems.

Emanuel di Pasquale teaches at Middlesex County College in Edison, New Jersey. His poems have appeared in many magazines and anthologies. His latest book is *Cartwheel to the Moon.* "My Brother Loves Small Animals" first appeared in *Poems for Brothers, Poems for Sisters,* selected by Myra Cohn Livingston.

Rebecca Kai Dotlich's books for young readers include *When Riddles Come Rumbling: Poems to Ponder* and *A Family Like Yours.* "The Two of Us" is an original poem. "You and Me" first appeared in *Climb into My Lap: First Poems to Read Together,* edited by Lee Bennett Hopkins.

Lois Duncan is the award-winning author of more than fifty books, ranging from picture books to adult novels. She is best known for her young-adult suspense novels. "Song of Frustration" is from her book *Spring to Spring.*

Eleanor Farjeon was a well-known English poet, playwright, and songwriter. She won the Hans Christian Andersen medal for her body of work in 1956. "The Quarrel," her poem in this book, came from her book *Silver, Sand and Snow.*

Karama Fufuka is the author of many poems and stories for children. "Lil' Bro'" comes from her book *My Daddy Is a Cool Dude and Other Poems.*

Kristine O'Connell George received the Lee Bennett Hopkins Promising Poet Award from the International Reading Association in 1998. "Hide and Go Seek," her poem in this book, comes from her book *Old Elm Speaks: Tree Poems.*

Nikki Grimes has had many poems, articles, essays, editorials, and photographs published. She has written several books for young people, including the poetry book *Something on My Mind.*

David L. Harrison is the author of numerous books, including *The Book of Giant Stories,* winner of the Christopher Award, and several books of poetry. "Who Ate the Last Five Cookies?" comes from his book *A Thousand Cousins: Poems of Family Life.*

Mary Ann Hoberman is a recipient of the National Council of Teachers of English Award for Excellence in Poetry for Children. Her works for young readers include the award-winning book *A House Is a House for Me.* "Half-Whole-Step" comes from her book *Fathers, Mothers, Sisters, Brothers: A Collection of Family Poems.*

Sara Holbrook is a noted poet whose many books include *Wham! It's a Poetry Jam: Discovering Performance Poetry* and *By Definition: Poems of Feelings.* "My Brother" comes from her poetry book *Nothing's the End of the World.*

J. Patrick Lewis has written many children's books, including *Doodle Dandies: Poems That Take Shape* and *A Burst of Firsts: Doers, Shakers, and Record Breakers.* "Sister and Bro" is an original poem.

Richard J. Margolis was an award-winning journalist, essayist, and poet. "Birthday" comes from his book of poems *Secrets of a Small Brother.*

Jane Medina's poetry reflects her dedication to children and their education during her more than twenty years as an elementary-school teacher. She is the author of the poetry book *My Name Is Jorge: On Both Sides of the River.* "I'm Telling" is an original poem.

John Micklos, Jr., has written about educational issues for more than twenty years. His books include *Daddy Poems, Mommy Poems,* and *Grandparent Poems.* "New Baby Sister," "Don't You Tease My Sister," "No Boys Allowed," and "Bunk Bed Dreams" are original poems.

Eileen Spinelli is the author of many picture books and books of poetry, including *When Mama Comes Home Tonight* and *Tea Party Today: Poems to Sip and Savor.* "Big Sister, Good-bye" is an original poem.

William Wise's poem "My Little Sister" first appeared in his book of poems *All on a Summer's Day.*

Acknowledgments

Every effort has been made to trace the ownership of each poem included in *No Boys Allowed*. If any errors or omissions have occurred, corrections will be made in subsequent printings, provided the publisher is notified of their existence. We gratefully acknowledge those who granted permission to use the poems that appear in this book.

Boyds Mills Press, Inc., for "Who Ate the Last Five Cookies?" from *A Thousand Cousins: Poems of Family Life* by David L. Harrison, published by Boyds Mills Press, Inc. Text copyright © 1996 by David L. Harrison; "My Brother" from *Nothing's the End of the World* by Sara Holbrook, published by Boyds Mills Press, Inc. Text copyright © 1995 by Sara Holbrook. Reprinted by permission.

Clarion Books for "Hide and Go Seek" from *Old Elm Speaks* by Kristine O'Connell George. Text copyright © 1998 by Kristine O'Connell George. Reprinted by permission of Clarion Books, an imprint of Houghton Mifflin Company. All rights reserved.

Curtis Brown, Ltd., for "The Two of Us" by Rebecca Kai Dotlich. Copyright © 2004 by Rebecca Kai Dotlich; "You and Me" by Rebecca Kai Dotlich. Copyright © 1998 by Rebecca Kai Dotlich. First appeared in *Climb into My Lap: First Poems to Read Together*, edited by Lee Bennett Hopkins, published by Simon & Schuster Books for Young Readers; "little sister" from *Something on My Mind* by Nikki Grimes, published by Dial Books for Young Readers. Copyright © 1978 by Nikki Grimes; "My Little Sister" from *All on a Summer's Day* by William Wise, published by Pantheon. Copyright © 1971 by William Wise. Reprinted by permission of Curtis Brown, Ltd.

David Higham Associates for "The Quarrel" from *Silver, Sand and Snow* by Eleanor Farjeon, published by Michael Joseph. Reprinted by permission of David Higham Associates.

Allan A. De Fina for "I'm Still Getting Used to My Little Brother" and "My Older Sister's in the Bathroom" by Allan A. De Fina. Copyright © 2004 by Allan A. De Fina. Used by permission of the author.

Dial Books for Young Readers for "Lil' Bro'" from *My Daddy Is a Cool Dude and Other Poems* by Karama Fufuka. Copyright © 1975 by Karama Fufuka. Used by permission of Dial Books for Young Readers, an imprint of Penguin Putnam Books for Young Readers, a division of Penguin Putnam, Inc. All rights reserved.

Emanuel di Pasquale for "My Brother Loves Small Animals" by Emanuel di Pasquale. Copyright © 1991 by Emanuel di Pasquale. First appeared in *Poems for Brothers, Poems for Sisters*, compiled by Myra Cohn Livingston, published by Holiday House. Reprinted by permission of the author.

G. P. Putnam's Sons for "Little" from *Everything and Anything* by Dorothy Aldis. Copyright © 1925–1927, renewed 1953, © 1954, 1955 by Dorothy Aldis. Used by permission of G. P. Putnam's Sons, an imprint of Penguin Putnam Books for Young Readers, a division of Penguin Putnam, Inc. All rights reserved.

J. Patrick Lewis for "Sister and Bro" by J. Patrick Lewis. Copyright © 2004. Used by permission of the author.

Little, Brown and Company, Inc., for "Half-Whole-Step" from *Fathers, Mothers, Sisters, Brothers: A Collection of Family Poems* by Mary Ann Hoberman. Text copyright © 1991 by Mary Ann Hoberman. By permission of Little, Brown and Company, Inc.

Margolis & Associates for "Birthday" from *Secrets of a Small Brother* by Richard J. Margolis, published by Macmillan. Copyright © 1984 by Richard J. Margolis. Reprinted by permission of Margolis & Associates.

Jane Medina for "I'm Telling" by Jane Medina. Copyright © 2004 by Jane Medina. Used by permission of the author.

John Micklos, Jr., for "Bunk Bed Dreams," "Don't You Tease My Sister," "New Baby Sister," and "No Boys Allowed" by John Micklos, Jr. Copyright © 2004 by John Micklos, Jr. Used by permission of the author.

Eileen Spinelli for "Big Sister, Good-bye" by Eileen Spinelli. Copyright © 2004 by Eileen Spinelli. Used by permission of the author.

Sterling Lord Literistic for "Song of Frustration" from *Spring to Spring* by Lois Duncan, published by Westminster John Knox Press in 1982. Used by permission of Sterling Lord Literistic. All rights reserved.